I0606255

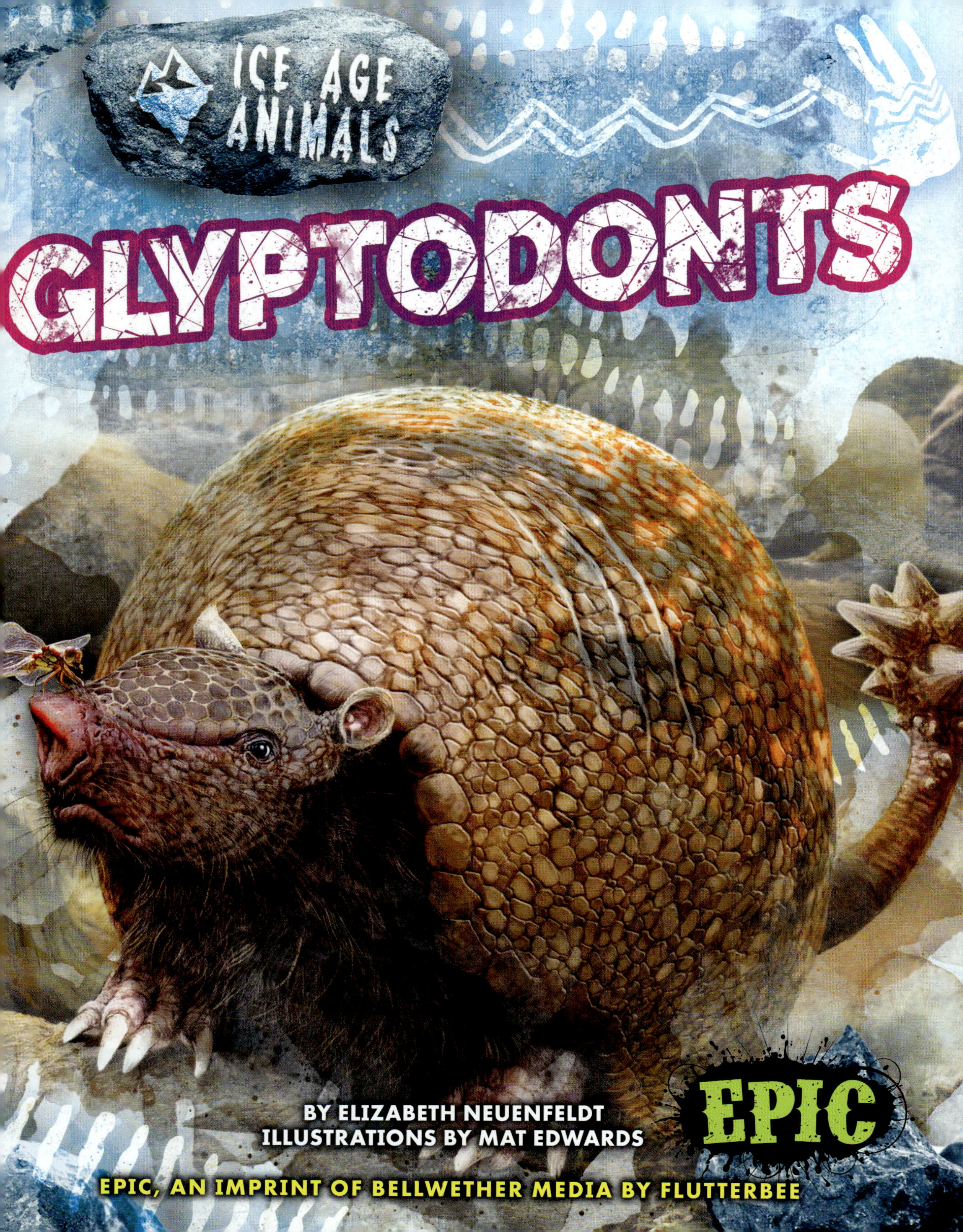
ICE AGE ANIMALS
GLYPTODONTS
BY ELIZABETH NEUENFELDT
ILLUSTRATIONS BY MAT EDWARDS
EPIC
EPIC, AN IMPRINT OF BELLWETHER MEDIA BY FLUTTERBEE

EPIC BOOKS are no ordinary books. They burst with intense action, high-speed heroics, and shadows of the unknown. Are you ready for an Epic adventure?

This edition first published in 2026 by Bellwether Media, Inc.

For information regarding permission, write to Bellwether Media, Inc., Attention: Permissions Department, 3500 American Blvd W, Suite 150, Bloomington, MN 55431.

Library of Congress Cataloging-in-Publication Data is available at www.loc.gov or upon request from the publisher.

ISBN: 9798893048179 (hardcover)
ISBN: 9798893049176 (ebook)

Editor: Betsy Rathburn   Designer: Jeffrey Kollock

Printed in the United States of America, North Mankato, MN.

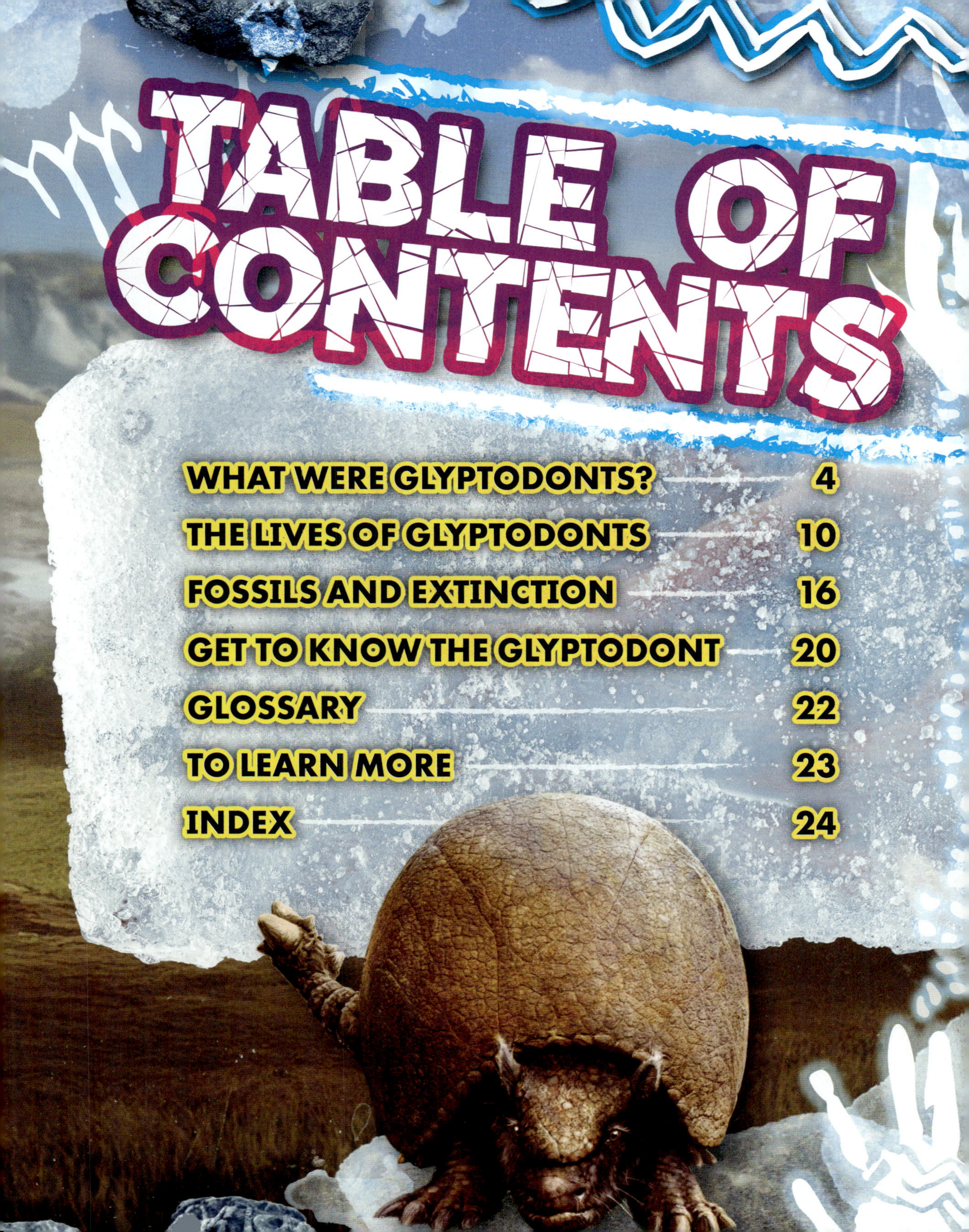

TABLE OF CONTENTS

WHAT WERE GLYPTODONTS? 4
THE LIVES OF GLYPTODONTS 10
FOSSILS AND EXTINCTION 16
GET TO KNOW THE GLYPTODONT 20
GLOSSARY 22
TO LEARN MORE 23
INDEX 24

WHAT WERE GLYPTODONTS?

Glyptodonts were **ancient** armadillos. These **mammals** lived in North and South America. They were known for their big shells!

Glyptodonts first appeared around 35 million years ago. This was during the Late **Eocene epoch**.

Glyptodonts were nearly 5 feet (1.5 meters) tall. They were up to 13 feet (4 meters) long!

GLYPTODONT SIZE COMPARISON

They had short legs and faces.
They had fur on their legs and faces.

Their backs had **rigid** shells. These were made of **scutes**. Shells kept them safe from **predators**.

THICK ARMOR

This animal's scutes could be over 1 inch (2.5 centimeters) thick!

They had strong tails. Some tails had spikes at the end!

THE LIVES OF GLYPTODONTS

Glyptodonts lived in many **habitats**. They lived in forests and mountains. They often lived near water.

Many glyptodonts were **herbivores**. They ate plants such as grasses and bushes. Some were **omnivores**. They also ate **insects**.

Glyptodonts dug **burrows** with their claws. They likely spent their days inside their burrows. They came out at sunset.

Males likely fought one another for **territory**.

Early humans hunted glyptodonts. Saber-toothed cats and dire wolves likely hunted them too.

Glyptodonts fought back. They attacked with their strong tails. Thick shells kept them safe from attacks.

FOSSILS AND EXTINCTION

Most glyptodonts died out around 10,000 years ago. They died from overhunting and changes in **climate**.

Many glyptodont **fossils** have been found. They help people learn how glyptodonts lived.

HUNTED GLYPTODONT
DATE FOUND
2024
WHERE
Reconquista River, Argentina
FAMOUS FOR
Fossil shell that shows humans hunted glyptodonts 21,000 years ago
SOUTH AMERICA

Glyptodonts are related to today's armadillos. Both animals have shells.
GLYPTODONT
spiked tail
thick, rigid shell
large body

Armadillos are smaller. They have thin, bendable shells. They have thin tails. Glyptodonts are gone. But their relatives live on!

GET TO KNOW THE GLYPTODONT

WHEN DID THEY LIVE?

around 35 million years ago

Glyptodonts first appear

160,000 to 90,000 years ago

Early modern humans first appear

around 10,000 years ago

Glyptodonts die out

WHO FAMOUSLY RECORDED AN EARLY FOSSIL?

Charles Darwin in the **1830s**

short face

HEIGHT

nearly 5 feet (1.5 meters) tall

WEIGHT

up to around 5,290 pounds (2,400 kilograms)

GLOSSARY

ancient–from long ago

burrows–holes or tunnels in the ground that some animals dig for homes

climate–the long-term weather in a particular place

Eocene epoch–a geological time period that began around 56 million years ago and ended around 33.9 million years ago; the Late Eocene epoch started around 38 million years ago.

fossils–the remains of living things that lived long ago

habitats–areas with certain types of plants, animals, and weather

herbivores–animals that only eat plants

insects–small animals with six legs and hard outer bodies; an insect's body is divided into three parts.

mammals–warm-blooded animals that have backbones and feed their young milk

omnivores–animals that eat both plants and animals

predators–animals that hunt other animals for food

rigid–not bendable

scutes–bony plates or scales that cover the bodies of some animals

territory–the land area where an animal lives

TO LEARN MORE

AT THE LIBRARY

Gleisner, Jenna Lee. *If I Camped with a Giant Armadillo.* Minneapolis, Minn.: Jump!, 2026.

Ruby, Rex. *Inside an Armadillo's Burrow.* Minneapolis, Minn.: Bearport Publishing Company, 2023.

Shreeve, Elizabeth. *The Oddball Book of Armadillos.* New York, N.Y.: W. W. Norton & Company, 2024.

ON THE WEB

FACTSURFER

Factsurfer.com gives you a safe, fun way to find more information.

1. Go to www.factsurfer.com.
2. Enter "glyptodonts" into the search box and click 🔍.
3. Select your book cover to see a list of related content.

INDEX

armadillos, 4, 18, 19
burrows, 12
Eocene epoch, 5
fighting, 13, 15
food, 11
fossils, 16, 17
get to know, 20–21
habitats, 10
name, 5
predators, 8, 9, 14
range, 4, 5
shells, 4, 8, 15, 17, 18, 19
size, 6, 19
tails, 9, 15, 18, 19

The images in this book are reproduced through the courtesy of: Mat Edwards, front cover, pp. 1, 4-5, 6-7, 8-9, 10-11, 12-13, 14-15, 16-17, 18-19, 20-21.